# Mastering Kitchen Fundamentals:

A Beginner's Guide to Culinary Excellence

By Raymone Keitt

All rights reserved. Reproduction in whole or in part without written permission is prohibited

**Table of Contents**

Introduction *4*

Chapter 1: Essential Kitchen Tools *5*

Chapter 2: Knife Skills *11*

Chapter 3: Cutting Boards *14*

Chapter 4: Measuring and Mixing *19*

Chapter 5: Cooking Pans and Sheets *26*

Chapter 6: Essential Cooking Utensils *31*

Chapter 7: Specialized Kitchen Tools *34*

Chapter 8: Cleaning and Maintenance *37*

Chapter 9: Efficiency Techniques *40*

Chapter 10: Budget-Friendly Kitchen Setup *43*

Chapter 11: The Final Course *47*

Appendix *60*

Recipes to get you started *66*

Acknowledgements *76*

About the Author *77*

Index *79*

# Introduction

Welcome to the World of Cooking

Cooking is more than just preparing meals; it's an art, a science, and a deeply rewarding journey. Whether you're a novice in the kitchen or an experienced home cook, mastering the fundamentals is the first step toward culinary excellence. In "Mastering Kitchen Fundamentals: A Beginner's Guide to Culinary Excellence," we embark on this exciting journey together.

This book is designed to be your trusted companion, guiding you through the essential tools, techniques, and skills that will empower you to create delicious dishes with confidence and creativity. From selecting the right knives to mastering precise measurements, from efficient pan usage to understanding the role of specialized tools, we'll cover it all. By the end of this book, you'll not only know your way around the kitchen but also have the knowledge to elevate your cooking to a whole new level.

Cooking should be a joyous adventure, an opportunity to express your creativity, and a way to savor the flavors of the world. It's about transforming simple ingredients into unforgettable meals that bring joy to your table and those you share it with. Whether you're cooking for yourself, your family, or guests, the fundamentals you'll learn here are the foundation for culinary success.

In these pages, you'll discover the art of precise measurements, the satisfaction of mastering knife skills, the efficiency of proper pan usage, and the joy of creating flavorful dishes. We'll explore the importance of maintaining your kitchen tools, budget-friendly ways to set up your kitchen, and how to continue your culinary journey beyond this book.

So, let's roll up our sleeves, put on our aprons, and dive headfirst into the exciting world of cooking. By the end of this journey, you'll not only be a skilled home chef but also a culinary enthusiast eager to explore new cuisines, techniques, and flavors.

Whether you're here to embark on a lifelong culinary adventure or simply want to improve your cooking skills, this book is your guide to mastering kitchen fundamentals. Let's get started and unlock the delicious potential that lies within your kitchen.

Happy cooking!

Raymone Keitt

Author of "Mastering Kitchen Fundamentals: A Beginner's Guide to Culinary Excellence"

## Chapter 1: Essential Kitchen Tools

**Understanding the Basic Tools**

On your path to greatness in the world of culinary arts, knowledge is power, but having the right tools at your disposal is equally important. Before you embark on your cooking journey, it's crucial to understand the basic kitchen tools that will become your trusted companions. This chapter will introduce you to the fundamental kitchen tools that form the foundation of every great meal. From knives and cutting boards to measuring cups and pots, we'll explore the essential items you need to create delicious dishes.

1. Knives: Your culinary adventure begins with the knife. Knives are the heart and soul of the kitchen, used for chopping, dicing, slicing, and so much more. In this section, we'll explore various types of knives, from chef's knives for versatile cutting to paring knives for delicate work.

2. Cutting Boards: A reliable cutting board is where the magic happens. We'll discuss different materials, such as wood, plastic, and bamboo, and their pros and cons. You'll also learn how to maintain your cutting board for long-lasting use.

3. Measuring Cups and Spoons: Precision is key in cooking. Discover the importance of measuring cups and spoons in achieving consistent and delicious results. We'll cover dry measuring cups, liquid measuring cups, and various sizes of measuring spoons.

4. Pots and Pans: Versatile cookware is essential for a wide range of cooking methods. You'll learn about the basic pots and pans every kitchen should have, including saucepans, skillets, and stockpots.

5. Mixing Bowls: Mixing bowls are where ingredients come together. We'll explore their various sizes and materials, helping you choose the right bowl for each task, whether it's tossing a salad or mixing dough.

By understanding these basic kitchen tools, you'll lay a strong foundation for your culinary adventures. Each tool has its unique role and purpose, contributing to your efficiency and success in the kitchen.

**Investing in Quality: Why It Matters**

In the world of kitchen tools, the old adage "you get what you pay for" holds true. Investing in high-quality kitchen tools may require a larger upfront expense, but it pays off in the long run. Here's why the quality of your kitchen tools matters:

1. Durability: Quality kitchen tools are built to withstand the test of time. They are often made from superior materials and constructed with precision, ensuring they won't break or wear out quickly. When you invest in durable tools, you won't find yourself needing to replace them frequently.

2. Performance: The performance of your kitchen tools can significantly impact your cooking experience. High-quality knives stay sharp longer, cutting boards resist warping and staining, and cookware distributes heat evenly. These factors directly affect the quality of your dishes.

3. Safety: Safety should always be a top priority in the kitchen. Quality tools are designed with safety features in mind. Sharp knives are less likely to slip, and non-stick cookware with a sturdy handle is less likely to cause accidents.

4. Efficiency: Quality tools are designed to make your cooking tasks more efficient. A sharp knife will slice through ingredients with ease, saving you time and effort. Properly constructed cookware ensures even cooking, preventing food from sticking or burning.

5. Precision: Precision matters, especially in baking and more intricate cooking techniques. High-quality measuring cups and spoons provide precise measurements, while a good kitchen scale allows you to weigh ingredients accurately, resulting in consistent and reliable results.

6. Longevity: Quality tools have a longer lifespan. While cheaper options may seem attractive at first, they often need to be replaced sooner, which can end up costing you more in the long term. Quality tools can last for decades with proper care.

7. Enhanced Cooking Experience: Cooking should be an enjoyable experience, and quality tools can enhance that experience. They feel comfortable in your hand, perform predictably, and give you confidence in the kitchen.

When considering your kitchen tools, think of them as long-term investments in your culinary journey. By choosing quality over quantity, you'll not only elevate your cooking but also save money over time. Plus, cooking with reliable and efficient tools can be a truly satisfying experience.

As you build your collection of kitchen tools, prioritize quality for those items you'll use most frequently. For items you'll use less often, it's acceptable to opt for more budget-friendly alternatives, but for your essentials, it's wise to invest wisely.

**Building Your Essential Toolkit**

Now that we've emphasized the significance of quality kitchen tools, let's discuss the essential items that should find their way into your culinary arsenal. Consider this the foundation upon which you'll build your cooking skills and experiment with various recipes. Here are the key tools that every home cook should have:

1. Chef's Knife: The chef's knife is the workhorse of the kitchen. Its versatility makes it ideal for a wide range of tasks, from chopping and slicing to dicing and mincing. Invest in a high-quality chef's knife that feels comfortable in your hand.

2. Cutting Board: A durable and spacious cutting board is essential. While materials like plastic, bamboo, and wood each have their advantages, make sure it's large enough to comfortably prep ingredients without crowding.

3. Measuring Cups and Spoons: Precise measurements are crucial in cooking and baking. A set of measuring cups for both dry and liquid ingredients, along with measuring spoons, will ensure your recipes turn out as intended.

4. Kitchen Scale: For precise measurements, especially in baking, a kitchen scale is invaluable. It allows you to weigh ingredients to the gram, guaranteeing consistency in your dishes.

5. Cookware Set: A good cookware set includes a variety of pots and pans, typically with lids. Look for quality materials like stainless steel or non-stick coatings, ensuring even heat distribution and easy food release.

6. Sauté Pan or Skillet: A sauté pan or skillet with straight sides provides a larger cooking surface and is perfect for tasks like searing, stir-frying, and cooking dishes with more liquid.

7. Saucepan: A deeper pan with a lid, ideal for making sauces, soups, and boiling liquids. It excels at cooking delicate ingredients and liquids that require precise temperature control.

8. Baking Sheet: A flat, rimmed tray for baking cookies, biscuits, and other flat items. Parchment paper or silicone baking mats can be used to prevent sticking.

9. Mixing Bowls: A set of mixing bowls in various sizes is essential for combining and preparing ingredients.

10. Utensils: Essential kitchen utensils include spatulas, tongs, ladles, slotted spoons, and a whisk. These tools help you handle, flip, stir, and serve your culinary creations.

11. Blender or Food Processor: Choose one or both, depending on your cooking style. Blenders are excellent for smoothies, soups, and sauces, while food processors are versatile for chopping, slicing, and mixing.

12. Can Opener: An essential tool for accessing canned ingredients like tomatoes, beans, and more.

13. Peeler and Zester: These specialized tools make peeling and zesting fruits and vegetables a breeze.

14. Knife Sharpener or Honing Rod: To keep your knives in top shape, invest in a knife sharpener or honing rod for regular maintenance.

15. Oven Mitts: Protect your hands from hot cookware and dishes with heat-resistant oven mitts.

16. Kitchen Timer: Whether analog or digital, a kitchen timer ensures precise timing for your recipes.

Remember that this list serves as a starting point. As you gain confidence and expand your culinary repertoire, you may discover the need for additional tools and gadgets to suit your specific cooking interests. By building a solid foundation with these essential tools, you'll be well-prepared to explore the exciting world of culinary arts.

**Optional Tools for Aspiring Chefs**

While the essential kitchen tools we discussed earlier are the backbone of any home kitchen, there's a world of additional gadgets and appliances that can elevate your culinary adventures. These optional tools aren't essential for beginners but can greatly enhance your cooking and open up exciting possibilities as you grow as a chef. Here are some optional kitchen tools to consider:

1. Stand Mixer: A powerful stand mixer is a baker's best friend. It can handle tasks like kneading dough, whipping egg whites, and mixing batters with ease. While a hand mixer can suffice for many recipes, a stand mixer offers more power and hands-free operation.

2. Food Processor: For advanced meal prep and more intricate recipes, a food processor is a valuable addition. It excels at chopping, slicing, grating, and even making nut butters and dough.

3. Immersion Blender: Also known as a hand blender, this tool is perfect for pureeing soups and sauces directly in the pot. It's compact, easy to clean, and handy for blending small quantities.

4. Microplane Grater: If you enjoy adding zest to your dishes or grating ingredients like Parmesan cheese or nutmeg, a microplane grater is a precise and efficient tool.

5. Mandoline Slicer: Achieve uniform slices and julienne cuts effortlessly with a mandoline slicer. It's great for preparing dishes like potato gratin or thinly sliced vegetables for salads.

6. Digital Thermometer: For precise temperature control, especially when cooking meats, a digital thermometer is indispensable. It ensures your dishes are perfectly cooked every time.

7. Pressure Cooker: An electric pressure cooker can drastically reduce cooking times and tenderize tough cuts of meat. It's a versatile tool for busy cooks.

8. Sous Vide Machine: Popular among culinary enthusiasts, sous vide cooking involves vacuum-sealing ingredients in a bag and cooking them in a water bath at a precise temperature. It's perfect for achieving restaurant-quality results.

9. Smoking Gun: If you're interested in experimenting with smoking techniques, a smoking gun infuses dishes with smoky flavors without the need for a full-sized smoker.

10. Pasta Maker: If you love homemade pasta, a pasta maker lets you create various pasta shapes and sizes from scratch.

11. Kitchen Torch: For culinary adventures like caramelizing sugar on crème brûlée or torching meringue, a culinary blowtorch can be both fun and functional. Beyond dessert torching, a kitchen torch can be used for tasks like browning the top of casseroles or melting cheese on dishes.

Remember that these optional tools cater to specific culinary interests and techniques. As you gain experience and explore new recipes, you may find that one or more of these tools align with your cooking style and goals. They can certainly add a layer of creativity and precision to your culinary endeavors. However, there's no rush to acquire them all at once. Take your time, experiment, and gradually expand your kitchen toolkit as your skills and passion for cooking grow.

In the subsequent chapters of this book, we will dive deeper into each of these essential and optional kitchen tools in more detail, exploring their uses, care, and techniques for efficient and enjoyable cooking. So, let's embark on this culinary journey, armed with the knowledge and tools you need to create delicious meals in your kitchen.

## Chapter 2: Knife Skills

### The Chef's Best Friend: A Good Knife

A good quality knife is the cornerstone of any well-equipped kitchen. It's your most valuable tool and a chef's best friend. The right knife will make your cooking tasks easier, more efficient, and even more enjoyable.

A Few Key Points:

Invest in a chef's knife: A chef's knife is a versatile, all-purpose knife that's ideal for slicing, dicing, chopping, and more. Look for a knife with a comfortable handle and a blade that feels balanced in your hand.

Quality matters: While it might be tempting to buy a cheap knife, investing in a high-quality knife will pay off in the long run. Quality knives are more durable, stay sharp longer, and provide better control.

### Knife Types and Their Uses

Understanding the different types of knives and their specific uses is essential for efficient cooking. Here are some common knives and their purposes:

1. Chef's Knife: As mentioned earlier, the chef's knife is your go-to, all-purpose knife. It's perfect for slicing, dicing, chopping, and even mincing.

2. Paring Knife: Paring knives are smaller and ideal for precise tasks like peeling fruits and vegetables, trimming, and creating intricate garnishes.

3. Utility Knife: This knife falls between a chef's knife and a paring knife in size. It's versatile and can handle various cutting tasks.

4. Serrated Bread Knife: With its serrated edge, this knife is designed for slicing through bread and delicate items like tomatoes without crushing them.

5. Boning Knife: A boning knife has a thin, flexible blade used for removing bones from meat and fish.

6. Santoku Knife: Originating from Japan, the Santoku knife is excellent for slicing, dicing, and chopping. It often features a shorter, wider blade than a traditional chef's knife.

Remember: Always choose the right knife for the task at hand to ensure precision and safety.

**Knife Safety: A Cut Above the Rest**

Safety is paramount when working with knives. Here are some essential knife safety guidelines:

1. Proper Grip: Hold the knife with a firm grip but without tensing your hand too much. Your thumb and index finger should rest on opposite sides of the blade near the bolster (the knife's front part).

2. Keep Fingers Tucked: When cutting, tuck your fingers under your non-cutting hand's knuckles to protect them from accidental cuts.

3. Sharp Blade: A sharp knife is safer than a dull one. Dull blades require more force and are more likely to slip, leading to accidents. Regularly sharpen your knives.

4. Cut Away: Always cut away from your body to avoid accidentally cutting yourself.

5. Use a Cutting Board: Place a cutting board under your work area to protect your countertop and provide a stable surface.

**Knife Skills: Slicing, Dicing, and Chopping**

Now that you have the right knife and understand safety, let's explore basic knife skills:

1. Slicing: Slice by pushing the knife blade forward while guiding it with your free hand's fingers. Use a claw grip to protect your fingers.

2. Dicing: To dice, start by slicing the ingredient into planks, then stack the planks and cut them into sticks. Finally, cut across the sticks to create cubes.

3. Chopping: For chopping, use a rocking motion by lifting the blade and allowing it to fall while moving it forward. Keep your fingers safely tucked away.

**Honing vs. Sharpening: Keeping Your Knives in Top Shape**

Knife maintenance is crucial to ensure your knives stay in top shape. Honing and sharpening are two distinct processes:

Honing: Honing involves using a honing rod to realign the edge of the blade, maintaining its sharpness be-  tween sharpening sessions. It doesn't remove material from the blade.

Sharpening: Sharpening, on the other hand, is a more intensive process that grinds the blade to create a new, sharp edge.  Sharpen your knives as needed, depending on use.

By mastering these knife skills and techniques, you'll become a more confident and efficient cook, and your kitchen endeavors will be a cut above the rest.

## Chapter 3: Cutting Boards

**Emphasizing the Importance of Cutting Boards in the Kitchen**

Cutting boards are the unsung heroes of any kitchen. These humble kitchen tools play a pivotal role in food preparation, and their significance cannot be overstated. Whether you're a seasoned chef or a home cook, cutting boards are your loyal companions in the culinary journey. Let's delve into why they are indispensable:

1. Surface Protection: Cutting boards shield your countertops and kitchen surfaces from the relentless onslaught of sharp knives. Without them, your countertops would bear the scars of countless chopping sessions, leading to damage and a shorter lifespan.

2. Hygiene and Food Safety: Cutting boards are your first line of defense against foodborne illnesses. They create a barrier that prevents direct contact between raw ingredients and surfaces. This separation is essential to avoid cross-contamination, where harmful bacteria from one food item can transfer to another.

3. Knife Preservation: Cutting on the right surface ensures that your knives remain sharp and efficient. Using knives on hard surfaces like glass or granite can quickly dull their edges, leading to frustration and more frequent sharpening.

4. Versatility: Cutting boards come in various materials, each suited for specific tasks. Wooden boards are excellent for delicate slicing, while plastic boards are easily sanitized. Bamboo boards are eco-friendly, and specialized boards like marble or glass are perfect for presentation.

5. Organization: Different cutting board colors or labels help you keep track of what you're cutting, preventing mix-ups between vegetables, meats, and other ingredients. This organization is vital for efficient and safe meal preparation.

6. Easy Cleanup: Cleaning up after using a cutting board is far simpler than scrubbing and sanitizing an entire countertop. It saves time and effort, making post-cooking cleanup a breeze.

7. Presentation: In addition to their practicality, cutting boards can be used for elegant food presentations. Placing a beautifully arranged array of cheeses, fruits, or charcuterie on a wooden or slate cutting board instantly elevates your culinary presentation.

In summary, cutting boards are the unsung heroes that ensure your kitchen functions smoothly, keeping your food safe, your knives sharp, and your countertops intact. Their importance goes far beyond being a mere kitchen accessory; they are essential tools that every cook relies on. So, treat your cutting boards with care and respect, and they will continue to serve you faithfully in your culinary adventures.

## Wooden Cutting Boards

Benefits:

- Knife-Friendly: Wooden boards are gentle on knife edges, helping them stay sharper for longer.

- Attractive Aesthetics: Wooden cutting boards often add a touch of elegance to your kitchen.

- Natural Antibacterial Properties: Certain types of wood, like maple, have natural antibacterial properties that can inhibit the growth of harmful microbes.

Considerations:

- Maintenance: Wooden boards require regular oiling to prevent drying and splitting.

- Absorption: Wood can absorb liquids and odors, so it's essential to clean them thoroughly after each use.

## Plastic Cutting Boards

Benefits:

- Dishwasher Safe: Most plastic cutting boards are dishwasher safe, making cleanup a breeze.

- Affordability: They are often more budget-friendly than wooden or bamboo boards.

- Variety: Plastic boards come in various colors, allowing you to designate specific boards for different types of ingredients (e.g., one for vegetables, one for meats).

Considerations:

- Knife Wear: Plastic boards can be tough on knife edges, leading to faster dulling.

- Stains and Odors: Over time, plastic boards may retain stains and odors, especially when used for strong-smelling ingredients.

**Bamboo Cutting Boards**

Benefits:

- Eco-Friendly: Bamboo is a highly renewable resource, making bamboo cutting boards an eco-conscious choice.

- Durability: Bamboo is exceptionally durable, with natural antimicrobial properties.

- Knife-Friendly: It's less harsh on knife edges compared to glass or stone boards.

Considerations:

- Maintenance: Bamboo boards need regular oiling to prevent cracking.

- Hardness: Some bamboo boards can be harder on knife edges than other wooden boards.

**Glass or Stone Cutting Boards**

Benefits:

- Hygiene: Glass and stone boards are non-porous and highly resistant to stains and odors.

- Durability: They are exceptionally durable and resistant to knife marks.

Considerations:

- Knife Wear: These boards are extremely harsh on knife edges and can lead to quick dulling.

- Loudness: Cutting on glass or stone can be noisy and potentially damaging to knives.

**Flexible Mats**

Benefits:

- Space-Saving: These thin, flexible mats are easy to store.

- Versatility: They can be used as a portable surface for chopping, slicing, or rolling out dough.

Considerations:

- Durability: Flexible mats may need frequent replacement as they wear out relatively quickly.

- Knife Wear: Like plastic boards, they can be tough on knife edges.

**Choosing the Right Cutting Board**

The choice of cutting board material largely depends on your preferences and needs. For versatility, having a mix of wooden and plastic boards is a good strategy. Wooden boards are great for gentler prep work, while plastic boards are excellent for handling raw proteins due to their ease of cleaning and sanitation.

Remember that proper maintenance, regular cleaning, and replacing worn-out boards are key to keeping your cutting boards in top condition and ensuring safe food preparation.

**Wooden and Bamboo Cutting Boards: Caring for Your Kitchen Allies**

Wooden and bamboo cutting boards are beloved for their aesthetics, knife-friendliness, and natural antibacterial properties. However, to keep them in top-notch condition and prevent drying or cracking, regular oiling is essential. Here are the oils you can use:

Mineral Oil

- For Wooden Boards: Food-grade mineral oil is a fantastic choice. It's odorless, tasteless, and safe for food contact. Regularly apply a generous amount to your wooden cutting board, allowing it to soak in overnight. Wipe off any excess oil the next day. This process helps maintain the board's moisture and prevents cracks.

Beeswax and Mineral Oil Blends

- For Wooden Boards: Many products on the market combine beeswax and mineral oil. These blends provide both sealing and moisturizing properties. They create a protective barrier on the surface while hydrating the wood.

Coconut Oil

- For Bamboo Boards: Coconut oil is an excellent option for bamboo cutting boards. It's all-natural, food-safe, and has a pleasant scent. Apply a thin layer of coconut oil to your bamboo board and let it sit for a few hours or overnight. Wipe off any excess.

Butcher Block Conditioner

- For Both Wooden and Bamboo Boards: You can find specialized butcher block conditioners made explicitly for cutting boards. These often contain a combination of mineral oil and waxes or beeswax. They offer excellent protection and hydration.

Remember to reapply oil or conditioner to your wooden or bamboo cutting boards every few weeks or as needed, depending on usage and the dryness of the environment. Proper maintenance ensures these kitchen staples stay in great shape, ready to assist you in your culinary adventures.

## Chapter 4: Measuring and Mixing

Measuring Cups and Spoons: Precision in the Kitchen

Measuring cups and spoons are essential kitchen tools used to accurately measure both dry and wet ingredients in cooking and baking. They come in various shapes and sizes, and their primary purpose is to ensure that you use the correct amount of ingredients, which is crucial for the success of your recipes. Let's break down measuring cups and spoons, including their differences, similarities, usage for wet and dry ingredients, and their importance:

A Few Key Points:

Consistency Matters: In baking, especially, slight variations in measurements can lead to vastly different results. Precise measurements help you achieve that perfect texture and flavor.

Volume vs. Weight: Ingredients can be measured by volume (using measuring cups) or weight (using a kitchen scale). While both methods are valid, weight measurements are often more accurate.

Differences:

Material: Both measuring cups and spoons can be made of various materials, including plastic, metal (typically stainless steel), glass, wood, or even silicone. Stainless steel and glass are popular for their durability and resistance to staining.

Design: Measuring cups and spoons may come in different designs. Measuring cups may come as nesting cups, collapsible cups, or single-unit cups. Nested cups save space when stored, while collapsible cups are portable and easy to store.

Measuring spoons may come with rounded or flat bottoms. Flat-bottomed spoons are ideal for leveling off dry ingredients like flour, whereas rounded spoons are better for liquids.

Sizes: Standard measuring cup sizes include 1 cup (240 mL), 1/2 cup (120 mL), 1/3 cup (80 mL), and 1/4 cup (60 mL). Some sets may include additional sizes like 2/3 cup or 3/4 cup.

Dry Measuring Cups:

Dry measuring cups are designed to be filled to the brim and leveled off for accurate measurements of dry ingredients like flour, sugar, or oats. Use a flat edge, like a knife or spatula, to level the ingredients.

-Avoid Packing: For ingredients like flour, resist the temptation to pack it down in the measuring cup. Simply scoop it in and level it off gently. Sometimes recipes call for packing ingredients such as Brown Sugar.

Remember that interchangeably using dry and liquid measuring cups can lead to inaccurate results. Using the right measuring tool for the job ensures your recipes turn out as intended, whether you're whipping up a batch of cookies or crafting a delectable sauce.

Measuring spoons are essential kitchen tools used to accurately measure both dry and wet ingredients in cooking and baking. They come in various shapes and sizes, and their primary purpose is to ensure that you use the correct amount of ingredients, which is crucial for the success of your recipes. Let's break down measuring spoons, including their differences, similarities, usage for wet and dry ingredients, and their importance:

**Differences**

Material: Measuring spoons can be made of different materials, including plastic, metal (usually stainless steel), or even wood. Stainless steel spoons are preferred for their durability and resistance to staining.

Shape and Size: Measuring spoons typically come in standard sizes: 1 tablespoon (15 mL), 1 teaspoon (5 mL), 1/2 teaspoon (2.5 mL), and 1/4 teaspoon (1.25 mL). Some sets also include odd sizes like 1/8 teaspoon or 3/4 teaspoon.

Design: Measuring spoons may have different designs, including rounded or flat bottoms. Flat-bottomed spoons are ideal for leveling off dry ingredients like flour, whereas rounded spoons are better for liquids.

Measuring spoons typically come in standard sizes: 1 tablespoon (15 mL), 1 teaspoon (5 mL), 1/2 teaspoon (2.5 mL), and 1/4 teaspoon (1.25 mL). Some sets also include odd sizes like 1/8 teaspoon or 3/4 teaspoon.

Similarities:

Accurate Measurements: All measuring cups and spoons are designed to provide precise measurements to ensure recipe consistency.

Handle: Both measuring cups and spoons feature a handle for easy pouring, holding, and make it easy to scoop and level off ingredients.

Wet vs. Dry Ingredients:

Measuring cups

Dry Ingredients: For dry ingredients like flour, sugar, or oats, use dry measuring cups. Fill the cup to overflowing, and then level it off with a flat edge (e.g., the back of a knife) for an accurate measurement.

Wet Ingredients: For wet ingredients like milk, oil, or yogurt, use liquid measuring cups. These cups typically have spouts and volume markings on the side. Fill the liquid to the desired measurement line at eye level for accuracy.

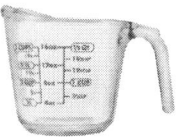

Measuring Spoons

Dry Ingredients: For dry ingredients like flour, sugar, or spices, fill the measuring spoon and level it off using a flat edge (e.g., the back of a knife) for an accurate measurement. Scoop the ingredient, and then level it to remove excess.

Wet Ingredients: For wet ingredients like oil, milk, or syrup, use a liquid measuring cup (with volume markings) rather than measuring spoons. Pour the liquid into the cup until it reaches the desired measurement line.

**How to Use Measuring Cups and Spoons:**

Dry Ingredients

Fill the measuring cup or spoon with the dry ingredient, allowing it to overflow slightly.

Level off the excess by sweeping a flat edge (e.g., a knife) across the top to create a level measurement.

Level Measurements: Ensure that your measurements are level, as a heaping spoonful or a partially filled spoon can affect the recipe's outcome.

Liquid ingredients

For Measuring cups pour the liquid ingredient into the measuring cup up to the desired measurement line. Check the measurement at eye level to ensure accuracy, as the meniscus (curved surface of the liquid) should align with the measurement line.

Use the Meniscus: The curvature formed by a substance in a measuring cup is called a meniscus, and it's created by surface tension on the top of the liquid. Measure from the lowest point of the curve for precision.

For measuring spoons pour ingredients to rim of spoon

Dry Before Reusing: If you're measuring both wet and dry ingredients in the same recipe, ensure that you dry the measuring cup or spoon thoroughly between uses to prevent any residue from affecting measurements.

Importance:

Recipe Consistency: Accurate measurements with measuring cups and spoons help maintain consistency in your recipes, ensuring that your dishes turn out as intended each time.

Baking Precision: Baking, in particular, relies heavily on precise measurements because slight variations can impact the texture and taste of the final product.

Proper Ratios: Measuring cups and spoons help you maintain the correct ratio of ingredients in your recipes, which is crucial for the success of your dishes.

Portion Control: Measuring cups and spoons also help with portion control, allowing you to manage your calorie intake and serving sizes.

Avoid Over/under seasoning: Measuring spoons are crucial for accurately adding spices and seasonings, preventing your dish from being too bland or overly seasoned.

Save Ingredients: Using measuring cups and spoons can help you avoid wasting ingredients by ensuring you only use the necessary amount.

In summary, measuring cups and spoons are indispensable tools in the kitchen, whether you're preparing a meal or baking. They provide accuracy, consistency, and control in your cooking, ensuring that your recipes turn out just right. Using the appropriate measuring cups and spoons for dry and wet ingredients is essential to achieve the best results in your culinary endeavors.

**Mixing Bowls**

Mixing bowls are essential tools in the kitchen that serve various purposes and play a crucial role in food preparation. They come in a variety of materials, each with its unique properties, and are available in different sizes to suit various cooking and baking needs. Here's an explanation of the importance of mixing bowls, differences in materials, examples of their uses, and maintenance tips:

Importance of Mixing Bowls:

Mixing Ingredients: Mixing bowls are primarily used for combining and blending ingredients, whether it's for baking, cooking, or making salads. They allow you to mix dry and wet ingredients, creating uniform and consistent mixtures.

Preparation: They are versatile tools for various kitchen tasks, such as marinating, tossing salads, and making sauces. Mixing bowls make it easy to prepare and store food before cooking.

Portioning: Mixing bowls come in various sizes, making it convenient to portion and measure ingredients for recipes accurately.

Temperature Control: Some mixing bowls can withstand high or low temperatures, allowing you to work with both hot and cold ingredients. This is especially important for tasks like melting chocolate or proofing yeast.

Differences in Materials:

Stainless Steel: Durable, easy to clean, and non-reactive, stainless steel mixing bowls are resistant to stains and odors. They are excellent for tasks that require temperature control.

Glass: Glass mixing bowls are transparent, allowing you to see the contents clearly. They are also non-reactive, so they won't affect the taste of your ingredients. However, they can be heavy and may break if dropped.

Plastic: Lightweight and affordable, plastic mixing bowls are perfect for casual use. They are less likely to break but may stain or absorb odors over time. Look for food-grade plastic options.

Ceramic: Ceramic mixing bowls are attractive and can be used for both mixing and serving. They come in various colors and designs but may be more fragile than other materials.

Copper: Copper mixing bowls are excellent for whipping egg whites, as copper reacts with the proteins in egg whites to create stable foam. They also look elegant in the kitchen.

Examples of Uses:

Baking: Mixing bowls are crucial for combining dry and wet ingredients when making cookies, cakes, bread, and other baked goods.

Salad Preparation: Use mixing bowls to toss and combine salad ingredients with dressings.

Marinating: Marinate meats, poultry, or tofu in mixing bowls to infuse flavor before cooking.

Making Sauces: Mixing bowls are ideal for making a wide range of sauces, from salad dressings to pasta sauces.

Storing Leftovers: Some mixing bowls come with lids, making them suitable for storing leftover food in the refrigerator.

Maintenance:

Cleaning: Wash mixing bowls immediately after use to prevent stains or odors from setting in. Most mixing bowls are dishwasher safe, but hand washing is often recommended to prolong their lifespan.

Stain Removal: To remove stains from plastic or ceramic bowls, make a paste of baking soda and water and scrub the stained areas. For stainless steel and glass, use a mixture of vinegar and water.

Avoid Abrasive Cleaners: Don't use abrasive scrubbers or cleaners on mixing bowls, as they can scratch the surface and affect their longevity.

Storage: Store your mixing bowls in a dry, cool place, and avoid stacking materials that might scratch or damage them.

Mixing bowls are fundamental tools in the kitchen, and choosing the right material and size for your specific needs can greatly enhance your cooking and baking experience. Proper care and maintenance will ensure they last for years.

## Chapter 5: Cooking Pans and Sheets

Cooking pans and sheets are like the unsung heroes of the kitchen. They come in various shapes, sizes, and materials, each designed for specific culinary tasks. Understanding the differences between them and selecting the right one can make a world of difference in your cooking adventures. In this chapter, we'll explore the diverse world of cooking pans and sheets, their characteristics, and the ideal uses for each.

**Skillet (Frying Pan)**

Versatile, Shallow, and Essential

The skillet, often referred to as a frying pan, is a kitchen workhorse. Its shallow, sloping sides and wide cooking surface make it perfect for various techniques, including frying, sautéing, searing, and even baking. Here's why it's indispensable:

- Even Heat Distribution: Skillets are known for their even heat distribution, ensuring that your food cooks uniformly.

- Non-Stick Options: Consider investing in a non-stick skillet for easy cooking and cleanup, especially when dealing with delicate items like eggs or fish.

Ideal Uses: Use skillets for frying eggs, searing steaks, sautéing vegetables, and making pancakes.

**Saucepan**

Deeper and Precise

A saucepan is a deeper pan with a lid, essential for preparing sauces, soups, and boiling liquids. Its design is perfect for cooking delicate ingredients that require precise temperature control. Here's why it's crucial:

Controlled Cooking: The depth and lid of a saucepan allow you to control the cooking process, making it ideal for simmering and reducing.

- Variety of Sizes: Saucepans come in various sizes, so you can choose the one that best suits your recipe.

Ideal Uses: Use saucepans for making sauces, soups, boiling pasta, and simmering dishes.

**Sauté Pan**

Straight Sided and Spacious

A sauté pan, also known as a sauté skillet, features straight sides and a larger cooking surface compared to a regular skillet. It's excellent for dishes with more liquid or when you need to contain ingredients effectively. Here's why it's valuable:

- More Room: Sauté pans provide ample space for stirring and flipping, making them ideal for dishes that involve tossing ingredients.

- Reduced Spillage: The straight sides help prevent spills when you're cooking items that release liquids.

Ideal Uses: Use sauté pans for stir-frying, sautéing vegetables, and cooking dishes with sauces or more liquid.

**Factors to Consider When Choosing a Pan**

Selecting the right pan involves considering factors such as material, size, and purpose. Here are some key considerations:

- Material: Stainless steel, non-stick, and cast iron are popular materials. Non-stick pans are great for easy cooking and cleaning, while cast iron provides excellent heat retention.

- Size: The size of the pan should match the recipe's quantity. A larger pan for smaller quantities may lead to uneven cooking.

- Purpose: Think about what you'll use the pan for most often. If you love searing steaks, a cast iron skillet is a must. If you frequently prepare sauces, a saucepan is essential.

In this chapter, we've scratched the surface of the world of cooking pans and sheets. Each type serves a unique purpose, and as you explore your culinary passions, you'll discover the importance of selecting the right one for the task at hand.

## Skillet (Frying Pan)

Dish: Pan-Seared Salmon with Lemon Butter Sauce

Description: A skillet is perfect for achieving that crispy, golden sear on the outside of salmon while keeping the inside tender and moist. The lemon butter sauce adds a burst of flavor.

Recipe:

1. Season salmon fillets with salt and pepper.

2. Heat the skillet over medium-high heat and add a bit of oil.

3. Place the salmon fillets in the skillet, skin side down (if applicable).

4. Sear for a few minutes until the skin is crispy and the salmon releases easily from the pan.

5. Flip the fillets and sear the other side until the salmon is cooked to your desired level of doneness.

6. In the same skillet, melt some butter and add lemon juice, garlic, and fresh herbs (like dill or parsley) to make the sauce.

7. Pour the lemon butter sauce over the seared salmon fillets and serve.

## Saucepan

Dish: Classic Tomato Soup

Description: A saucepan is perfect for simmering and reducing soups to perfection. Tomato soup is a classic comfort dish, and a saucepan helps in achieving the ideal consistency.

Recipe:

1. In a saucepan, sauté chopped onions and garlic in olive oil until they become translucent.

2. Add canned tomatoes, vegetable or chicken broth, salt, pepper, and a pinch of sugar to balance the acidity.

3. Simmer the mixture over medium-low heat, partially covered, for about 20-30 minutes to develop flavors.

4. Use an immersion blender directly in the saucepan to puree the soup until smooth.

5. Stir in heavy cream (if desired) and adjust seasoning.

6. Serve your delicious homemade tomato soup with a garnish of fresh basil.

**Sauté Pan**

Dish: Chicken Marsala

Description: A sauté pan provides ample space for sautéing chicken breasts and creating a rich Marsala wine sauce. The straight sides help contain the sauce and prevent spills.

Recipe:

1. Season chicken breasts with salt and pepper.

2. In the sauté pan, heat some olive oil and butter over medium-high heat.

3. Add the chicken breasts and cook until they are browned and cooked through. Remove them from the pan and set them aside.

4. In the same pan, add sliced mushrooms and minced shallots. Sauté until the mushrooms are tender.

5. Pour in Marsala wine and chicken broth, scraping up any browned bits from the bottom of the pan.

6. Let the sauce simmer and reduce until it thickens.

7. Return the cooked chicken breasts to the pan and simmer for a few more minutes.

8. Serve your Chicken Marsala over pasta or with mashed potatoes.

These dishes showcase the versatility and capabilities of the different pans. Whether you're searing, simmering, or sautéing, the right pan can make all the difference in achieving culinary success.

## Chapter 6: Essential Cooking Utensils

Cooking utensils are the unsung heroes of the kitchen, providing you with the means to mix, flip, stir, and serve your culinary creations. Whether you're a seasoned chef or a beginner in the culinary world, having the right utensils at your disposal can make a world of difference in your cooking endeavors. In this chapter, we'll explore the essential cooking utensils that every kitchen should have.

**Understanding the Role of Cooking Utensils**

Cooking utensils are tools designed to aid in food preparation, cooking, and serving. They come in various shapes, sizes, and materials, each serving a specific purpose in the kitchen. From spatulas and tongs to ladles and whisks, these utensils are indispensable for achieving the desired flavors, textures, and presentation of your dishes.

**The Must-Have Cooking Utensils**

1. Spatula

- Function: A spatula is a flat, flexible tool used for flipping, lifting, and turning foods. It's ideal for delicate items like pancakes, omelets, and fish fillets.

2. Tongs

- Function: Tongs are versatile, hinged utensils used for gripping and lifting food items. They excel in turning meats on a grill, tossing salads, and serving a variety of dishes.

3. Ladle

- Function: The ladle is a deep-bowled spoon with a long handle, primarily used for serving liquids and soups. Its deep bowl prevents spills and enables controlled pouring.

4. Slotted Spoon

- Function: Similar to a regular spoon, the slotted spoon has slots or holes that allow liquid to drain away. It's excellent for serving items like boiled eggs or retrieving foods from simmering liquids.

5. Whisk

- Function: A whisk is a hand tool with thin wires used for whipping, beating, and stirring. It's essential for achieving smooth batters, sauces, and dressings.

6. Wooden Spoon

 - Function: Wooden spoons are excellent for stirring and mixing in cookware without scratching the surface. They're ideal for use with non-stick pans.

7. Can Opener

- Function: Can openers are crucial for opening canned food items, providing access to ingredients like canned tomatoes, beans, or tuna.

8. Peeler

- Function: A peeler is designed to remove the skin from fruits and vegetables efficiently. It's essential for tasks like peeling potatoes, carrots, and cucumbers.

**Benefits of Choosing the Right Cooking Utensils**

Selecting the appropriate cooking utensils for your culinary tasks is essential for several reasons:

1. Efficiency: The right utensil can make tasks more efficient, saving you time and effort in the kitchen.

2. Safety: Using the correct utensil for a particular task minimizes the risk of accidents and injuries.

3. Preservation of Cookware: The choice of utensil can impact the longevity of your cookware, preventing scratches and damage.

4. Consistency: Proper utensils help you achieve consistent results in your dishes, ensuring that flavors and textures are as intended.

**Optional Utensils for Aspiring Chefs**

While the above list covers essential cooking utensils, there are many specialized utensils available that can elevate your cooking game. These optional utensils cater to specific cooking interests and techniques and include tools like mandoline slicers, microplane graters, and meat thermometers.

Remember that your choice of cooking utensils should align with your cooking style, preferences, and the types of dishes you frequently prepare. By having the right tools at your disposal, you'll find cooking more enjoyable and your culinary creations reaching new heights.

In the following chapters, we'll delve deeper into the usage and care of these essential and optional cooking utensils, ensuring that you're well-equipped and knowledgeable in your culinary adventures.

## Chapter 7: Specialized Kitchen Tools

While essential kitchen tools and utensils are the backbone of any kitchen, specialized tools cater to specific culinary tasks and techniques. These specialized kitchen tools can help you take your cooking to the next level, whether you're exploring new cuisines, experimenting with advanced techniques, or simply aiming for greater precision in your dishes.

In this chapter, we'll introduce you to a range of specialized kitchen tools and discuss their functions and applications.

Peeler

Function: A peeler is a tool designed for removing the skin or outer layer from fruits and vegetables. It excels in tasks like peeling potatoes, apples, cucumbers, and carrots.

Varieties: There are different types of peelers available, including Y-peelers, swivel peelers, and julienne peelers. Each type is suited for specific peeling tasks, so having a variety can be advantageous.

Zester

Function: A zester is a tool used to extract the flavorful zest (outermost layer) from citrus fruits such as lemons, limes, and oranges. It adds a burst of citrusy aroma and flavor to dishes, making them more vibrant and aromatic.

Varieties: Zesters come in various designs, including microplane graters and box graters. The choice depends on your preference and the level of zest fineness you desire.

Can Opener

Function: A can opener is a tool designed to open canned food items, providing access to ingredients like canned tomatoes, beans, or fruits.

Varieties: Can openers come in manual and electric versions. Manual can openers are more common and straightforward to use, while electric ones are powered and work with the push of a button.

Pizza Cutter

Function: A pizza cutter is a specialized wheel-like tool used for slicing pizzas into even portions. It can also be handy for cutting other flatbreads and pastry dough.

Varieties: Pizza cutters come in various sizes, and some have ergonomic handles for comfortable use.

Garlic Press

Function: A garlic press is a tool that finely minces garlic cloves, extracting their intense flavor. It's ideal for dishes that require the distinct taste of garlic without the texture of minced or chopped garlic.

Varieties: Garlic presses come in different designs, including handheld and press-and-roll styles.

Meat Tenderizer

Function: A meat tenderizer is a tool used to break down the fibers in tougher cuts of meat, making them more tender. It typically has a flat side for pounding and a textured side for tenderizing.

Varieties: Some meat tenderizers have dual-textured surfaces, while others are made of materials like stainless steel or mallet-style tenderizers.

Mortar and Pestle

Function: A mortar and pestle are used for grinding, mashing, and blending ingredients, especially spices, herbs, and small quantities of grains or seeds.

Varieties: Mortar and pestle sets are available in different materials, such as stone, marble, and wood. Each material can impart unique flavors and textures to your ingredients.

Kitchen Scale

Function: A kitchen scale is used for accurately measuring ingredients by weight, which is particularly important in baking and precision cooking.

Varieties: Kitchen scales can be analog or digital and come in various weight capacities. Digital scales are more precise and user-friendly.

These specialized kitchen tools open up new culinary possibilities, allowing you to explore a wider range of recipes and techniques. While they may not be considered essential for everyday cooking, they can greatly enhance your culinary adventures and help you achieve restaurant-quality results in your homemade dishes.

In the following sections, we'll delve into each of these specialized tools, exploring their usage, maintenance, and tips for getting the most out of them. Whether you're a novice or an experienced cook, these tools can elevate your culinary creations and inspire you to try new flavors and cooking styles.

## Chapter 8: Cleaning and Maintenance

A well-maintained kitchen is the heart of every home cook's domain. Just as a chef keeps their knives sharp and their workspace organized, you must also care for your kitchen tools and equipment to ensure they perform at their best. Proper cleaning and maintenance practices not only extend the life of your tools but also ensure safe food preparation. In this chapter, we'll explore the essential aspects of cleaning, maintaining, and storing your kitchen tools and equipment.

The Importance of Proper Cleaning

Cleaning your kitchen tools is not merely about aesthetics; it's about safety and functionality. Here's why proper cleaning matters:

1. Food Safety: Thoroughly cleaning your tools prevents the buildup of harmful bacteria, which can lead to foodborne illnesses.

2. Flavor Preservation: Residue from previous meals can alter the taste of your dishes. Cleaning ensures that your flavors remain pure.

3. Tool Longevity: Cleaning and drying tools promptly helps prevent rust and other forms of damage, prolonging their lifespan.

Cleaning Kitchen Tools by Material

Different materials require different cleaning methods. Here's how to clean tools made of common materials:

Stainless Steel

Stainless steel tools are durable and resistant to corrosion. To clean them:

- Use mild dish soap and warm water.

- Scrub with a soft sponge or cloth.

- Dry thoroughly to prevent water spots.

Plastic

Plastic tools are lightweight and affordable but can stain easily. Clean them by:

- Handwashing with mild soap.

- Avoid abrasive scrubbers to prevent scratches.

- Check for stains and address them promptly.

Wood

Wooden tools, like cutting boards and utensils, add a rustic charm to your kitchen but require special care:

- Hand-wash with mild soap, avoiding prolonged soaking.

- Dry thoroughly to prevent warping.

- Season cutting boards with food-grade mineral oil regularly.

Non-Stick

Non-stick cookware and utensils need gentle care to preserve their coating:

- Hand-wash with a soft sponge and mild soap.

- Avoid metal utensils that can scratch the non-stick surface.

- Use wooden or silicone utensils for cooking.

Safe Storage Practices

Proper storage is essential for keeping your kitchen tools in good condition:

- Store knives in a knife block or on a magnetic strip to protect their edges.

- Hang utensils or use utensil organizers for easy access.

- Use pan protectors or stack pans with paper towels between them to prevent scratches.

- Keep cutting boards flat to prevent warping.

Dishwasher-Safe Tools

Some kitchen tools and equipment are dishwasher-safe, but not all. Always refer to the manufacturer's instructions for guidance. In general, wooden, cast iron, and certain non-stick items should be hand-washed.

Special Care for Knives

Knives require extra attention:

- Hand-wash immediately after use with a mild detergent.

- Dry promptly to prevent water spots.

- Sharpen knives regularly to maintain their edge.

Delicate Tools

For delicate tools like wooden utensils and cast iron pans:

- Season cast iron pans to maintain their non-stick properties.

- Apply mineral oil to wooden tools to prevent drying and cracking.

Establishing a Cleaning Routine

To maintain an efficient and clean kitchen, establish a cleaning routine:

- Do quick cleaning after cooking to prevent food from hardening on surfaces.

- Schedule thorough cleaning sessions regularly.

- Tackle one area or tool at a time to avoid overwhelm.

By implementing these cleaning and maintenance practices, you'll ensure that your kitchen tools and equipment serve you well for years to come. A well-cared-for kitchen not only enhances your cooking experience but also promotes food safety and hygiene, making it a true haven for culinary exploration.

## Chapter 9: Efficiency Techniques

Efficiency in the kitchen is like a well-choreographed dance, where every move is purposeful, and every tool has its role. Whether you're a seasoned chef or a novice cook, mastering efficiency techniques can transform your cooking experience. In this chapter, we'll explore strategies and tips to streamline your cooking processes and enhance your culinary prowess.

**The Importance of Efficiency**

Efficiency in the kitchen is not just about saving time; it's about making cooking a more enjoyable and stress-free experience. Here's why it matters:

1. Time Savings: Efficient cooking means spending less time in the kitchen, which is especially valuable in today's fast-paced world.

2. Consistency: Efficiency techniques help ensure consistent results in your dishes.

3. Reduced Stress: By knowing how to navigate your kitchen effectively, you can cook with confidence and peace of mind.

**Knife Efficiency**

Efficiency starts with your knife skills:

- Use the Right Knife: Different knives are designed for specific tasks. Choose the appropriate one for chopping, slicing, or dicing.

- Master Knife Techniques: Learn techniques like the "claw grip" to hold ingredients safely and efficiently while chopping.

- Keep Your Knives Sharp: Dull knives require more force, making them less efficient and potentially dangerous.

**Blender Efficiency**

Efficient blending can save time and produce better results:

- Layer Ingredients: Add liquids first, followed by solids, to ensure smoother blending.

- Blend in Batches: If you're making large quantities, blend in batches rather than overloading the blender.

- Pulse Technique: Use short pulses for control when blending ingredients to avoid over-processing.

**Cookware Efficiency**

Efficient use of pots and pans can make a significant difference:

- Preheat Pans: Always preheat your pans before adding ingredients. This ensures even cooking and prevents sticking.

- Avoid Overcrowding: Overcrowding a pan can lead to uneven cooking. Use a larger pan or cook in batches when necessary.

- Maintain Proper Heat: Adjust heat levels during cooking to prevent burning or overcooking.

Measuring Efficiency

Efficient measuring is crucial for accurate recipes:

- Dry vs. Wet Measuring: Use dry measuring cups for ingredients like flour and sugar, and liquid measuring cups for liquids like milk or oil.

- Level Dry Ingredients: When measuring dry ingredients, level them off with a flat edge for accuracy.

- Zero-In on Accuracy: Precision in measuring ingredients can make a significant difference in the outcome of your dishes.

**Maintaining Tools for Efficiency**

Efficiency also means keeping your tools in top shape:

- Regular Sharpening: Maintain sharp knives for effortless cutting.

- Clean Blender Blades: Ensure blender blades are clean and free from residue for optimal blending.

- Season Cast Iron: Regularly season your cast iron pans to maintain their non-stick properties.

**Organized Workspace**

Efficiency begins with an organized workspace:

- Tools Within Reach: Keep frequently used tools within easy reach to avoid unnecessary movement.

- Clear Workspaces: A clutter-free workspace allows for smoother transitions between tasks.

- Clean as You Go: Minimize cleanup at the end by tidying up as you cook.

By incorporating these efficiency techniques into your culinary routine, you'll find yourself not only cooking with ease and precision but also gaining more time to savor the delightful results of your kitchen adventures. Efficiency is the secret ingredient that turns ordinary meals into extraordinary experiences.

## Chapter 10: Budget-Friendly Kitchen Setup

Cooking is a delightful journey, but it doesn't have to break the bank. In this chapter, we'll explore how to set up your kitchen with essential tools and equipment without emptying your wallet. Whether you're a student, a novice cook, or simply looking to save money, these budget-friendly tips will help you create a functional and efficient kitchen.

### The Importance of Budget-Friendly Setup

Setting up a budget-friendly kitchen is about making smart choices without compromising on quality or functionality. Here's why it's essential:

1. Financial Savings: A budget-friendly approach saves you money that can be better spent elsewhere.

2. Resourcefulness: It encourages creativity and resourcefulness in finding affordable solutions.

3. Accessibility: A well-equipped kitchen doesn't have to be expensive, making cooking accessible to more people.

### Identifying Essential Kitchen Tools

Begin by identifying the essential kitchen tools necessary for basic cooking tasks. These tools are the foundation of your kitchen setup:

- Quality Chef's Knife: A good quality chef's knife is versatile and essential for most cutting tasks.

- Cutting Board: Invest in a sturdy cutting board to protect your countertops and extend the life of your knives.

- Basic Cookware: Start with a few pots and pans, preferably non-stick, to cover various cooking techniques.

- Measuring Tools: Get measuring cups and spoons for accurate ingredient portions.

**Budget-Friendly Alternatives**

Now, let's delve into budget-friendly alternatives for these essential tools:

1. Secondhand Stores: Explore thrift shops, secondhand stores, or garage sales for quality kitchen tools at a fraction of the cost. You might find gently used knives or cookware in excellent condition.

2. Online Marketplaces: Websites like eBay or Facebook Marketplace often have kitchen tools available at discounted prices. Be sure to research the seller and read reviews for a secure transaction.

3. Basic and Multipurpose Tools: Start with basic and multipurpose tools that cover various tasks. For instance, a chef's knife can handle most cutting needs, and a versatile pot can be used for boiling, simmering, and frying.

**DIY Solutions**

Get creative with do-it-yourself (DIY) solutions for kitchen gadgets:

- Mason Jar Blender: Use a mason jar as a blender jar by attaching it to the blender's base. It's perfect for making smoothies and small batches of sauces.

- Glass Jar Storage: Repurpose glass jars from sauces, jams, or pickles as storage containers for dry goods like rice, pasta, or spices. Label them for easy identification.

- Homemade Potholders: Create potholders from old fabric or towels. They're practical and environmentally friendly.

**Cookware Choices**

For cookware, here are some budget-friendly options:

- Non-Stick Pans: Affordable non-stick pans are suitable for most cooking tasks and are easy to clean.

- Stainless Steel Pots: Stainless steel pots are durable and versatile, perfect for boiling, simmering, and making soups.

- Cast Iron Skillets: While cast iron skillets require some maintenance, they're long-lasting and offer excellent heat retention.

**Ingredient-Based Cooking**

Consider adopting an ingredient-based cooking approach. This means focusing on simple, affordable ingredients like grains, legumes, vegetables, and seasonal produce. With these staples, you can create flavorful and budget-friendly meals.

Here's an example of Ingredient-Based Cooking with a simple and budget-friendly recipe:

Chickpea and Vegetable Stir-Fry

Ingredients:

- 1 can of chickpeas (15 oz), drained and rinsed

- 2 cups of mixed vegetables (e.g., bell peppers, broccoli, carrots), chopped

- 1 onion, thinly sliced

- 2 cloves of garlic, minced

- 2 tablespoons of vegetable oil

- 2 tablespoons of soy sauce

- 1 teaspoon of ginger, grated (optional)

- Salt and pepper to taste

- Cooked rice or noodles (optional, for serving)

Instructions:

1. Heat a large skillet or wok over medium-high heat and add the vegetable oil.

2. Add the sliced onion and minced garlic to the skillet. Stir-fry for 2-3 minutes until they start to soften and become fragrant.

3. Add the chopped mixed vegetables to the skillet. Stir-fry for another 4-5 minutes until they begin to soften but are still crisp.

4. If you're using ginger, add it to the skillet and stir-fry for an additional minute to release its flavors.

5. Add the drained chickpeas to the skillet and stir-fry for 2-3 minutes to heat them through.

6. Drizzle the soy sauce over the mixture and toss everything together. Season with salt and pepper to taste. Continue to stir-fry for another 2 minutes, ensuring the ingredients are well-coated with the sauce.

7. Taste the stir-fry and adjust the seasoning if needed.

8. Serve your chickpea and vegetable stir-fry over cooked rice or noodles if you like.

This recipe is not only delicious but also budget friendly as it primarily relies on affordable ingredients like canned chickpeas and mixed vegetables. Feel free to customize it by adding your favorite spices or sauces. It's a quick and nutritious meal that showcases the versatility of staple ingredients while keeping your budget in check.

**Budget Planning**

Lastly, set a budget for your kitchen setup. Allocate funds for essential tools, prioritize quality where it matters most, and consider long-term investments. By planning your budget, you can make informed choices that align with your financial goals.

Setting up a budget-friendly kitchen doesn't mean sacrificing the joy of cooking. It's about making thoughtful choices and finding innovative solutions to create a kitchen that serves you well without straining your finances. With the right tools and resourcefulness, you can embark on a culinary adventure without breaking the bank.

## Chapter 11: The Final Course

**Culinary Exploration**

Congratulations! You've embarked on a journey through the fundamentals of the kitchen, mastering essential tools, and honing your culinary skills. Now, as we delve into Chapter 11, we're stepping into the world of culinary exploration, setting goals, and continuous learning. This chapter is your gateway to creativity and limitless possibilities in the kitchen and beyond.

Throughout the course of this book, you've laid a solid foundation by understanding the tools of the trade, learning efficient techniques, and even discovering budget-friendly ways to set up your kitchen. But cooking isn't just about following recipes; it's about expressing yourself, experimenting, and pushing the boundaries of your culinary prowess.

In this final chapter, we'll encourage you to explore beyond the basics. We'll discuss the value of curiosity, the importance of embracing mistakes as opportunities for growth, and how to expand your horizons by trying new cuisines and cooking styles. We'll also delve into the joy of sharing your culinary experiences and the benefits of connecting with fellow cooking enthusiasts.

Remember, the kitchen is your canvas, and ingredients are your palette. Whether you're an aspiring chef or simply someone who enjoys preparing meals at home, there's always room for exploration and innovation.

The Art of Culinary Exploration

In the world of culinary arts, the path to culinary mastery is paved with adventure and curiosity. Culinary exploration is not just a journey; it's a voyage into a realm of endless possibilities, where flavors, techniques, and cultures intertwine to create a symphony for the senses. As we delve into the art of culinary exploration, we discover the joy of discovery, the thrill of innovation, and the profound connection between food and the human experience.

Unleash Your Inner Explorer

Picture yourself as a fearless explorer, embarking on a grand expedition into uncharted culinary territory. Like any explorer, you must be equipped with the right tools, including a sense of wonder, an adventurous spirit, and a willingness to step outside your culinary comfort zone. Don your apron, wield your knife, and set sail into the vast sea of flavors and ingredients.

Embrace Diversity

Culinary exploration is a celebration of diversity. It's an opportunity to savor the world's rich tapestry of cuisines. From the vibrant street food of Bangkok to the comforting stews of Morocco, each culture offers its unique treasures waiting to be discovered. Don't be hesitant to explore global cuisine, for every bite is a step into a different world.

Experimentation: The Heart of Discovery

One of the most beautiful aspects of culinary exploration is experimentation. Dare to be different, and break free from the confines of recipes. Combine unusual ingredients, experiment with various cooking methods, and let your palate be your guide. Some of history's greatest culinary creations were born from the spirit of experimentation.

Local Bounty and Seasonal Sensibility

Culinary exploration need not be a journey to far-flung lands; it can begin in your local farmers' market. Discover the magic of seasonal produce and the joy of cooking with ingredients that are at the peak of freshness. As you explore what's available, you'll uncover a deeper connection to your own region's flavors.

Preserving Tradition, Creating Innovation

The balance between preserving culinary traditions and fostering innovation is the essence of culinary exploration. Don't forget the classics, but don't be afraid to give them a modern twist. Innovation is the heartbeat of the culinary world, pushing the boundaries of what's possible.

## From Fork to Farm

Culinary exploration isn't just about cooking; it's also about understanding where our food comes from. Visit local farms, dairies, and fisheries to see the origin of your ingredients. The connection to your food's source adds depth to your culinary journey.

## The Journey Is the Destination

Remember that culinary exploration is not just about the final dish but the entire process. Enjoy the experience of shopping for ingredients, the art of preparation, the anticipation as your creation simmers on the stove, and the satisfaction of sharing your culinary discoveries with others. It's a journey that engages all your senses.

## A Call to Adventure

Culinary exploration is an open invitation to every kitchen adventurer, novice, or expert. It's an ever-evolving voyage that offers new horizons at every turn. As you explore and experiment, you'll build your repertoire, enhance your skills, and deepen your appreciation for the culinary arts.

Now, don your chef's hat, gather your culinary compass, and set out on a path of endless possibilities. Each dish you create is a story waiting to be told, a memory to be cherished, and a step further on your journey of culinary exploration. Bon appétit!

## Embracing Curiosity, Mistakes, and Culinary Diversity

In the world of culinary arts, curiosity is the compass that guides us through uncharted gastronomic territories. It's the key to unlocking new flavors, techniques, and cultural experiences. In this chapter, we'll explore the value of curiosity, the importance of embracing mistakes as opportunities for growth, and how to expand your horizons by trying new cuisines and cooking styles.

## The Virtue of Curiosity

Curiosity is the driving force behind culinary exploration. It's the insatiable desire to know more, taste more, and create more. Here's why curiosity is invaluable in the culinary world:

1. Endless Learning: Curiosity fuels a never-ending journey of learning. Whether you're an amateur cook or a seasoned chef, there's always something new to discover, a fresh ingredient to explore, or an unfamiliar technique to master.

2. Innovation: Curious minds are the cradles of culinary innovation. The desire to experiment, combine, and reimagine ingredients and flavors often leads to the creation of extraordinary dishes.

3. Cultural Appreciation: Curiosity about the world's diverse cuisines and culinary traditions helps us appreciate the rich tapestry of global cultures. It fosters respect for different ways of life and the interconnectedness of food and humanity.

Embrace Mistakes as Stepping Stones

Mistakes in the kitchen are not failures but stepping stones on the path to culinary mastery. Here's why it's important to embrace errors as opportunities for growth:

1. Learning Experience: Mistakes offer a profound learning experience. When a recipe doesn't turn out as expected, take a moment to analyze what went wrong and learn from it.

2. Creativity Unleashed: Many culinary innovations were born from mistakes. Embracing errors can lead to new discoveries and inventive cooking techniques.

3. Resilience and Adaptation: Embracing mistakes in the kitchen builds resilience and adaptability. It teaches you to think on your feet, adapt to unforeseen circumstances, and find creative solutions.

4. Humility: Mistakes humble us and remind us that no one, not even the most renowned chefs, is infallible. Humility is a cornerstone of culinary growth.

Expanding Horizons Through Culinary Diversity

One of the most rewarding aspects of culinary exploration is trying new cuisines and cooking styles. Here's how to expand your horizons:

1. Local Ethnic Eateries: Seek out local ethnic restaurants or food trucks to try dishes from different cultures. Engaging your taste buds in this way is like a mini-vacation without leaving your town.

2. Cooking Workshops: Participate in cooking workshops or classes that focus on a specific cuisine. Learning from experienced chefs and cooks is a hands-on way to explore new cooking styles.

3. International Ingredients: Visit international grocery stores or markets and purchase ingredients you've never used before. Challenge yourself to create a dish around these unfamiliar elements.

4. Cooking Challenges: Host cooking challenges with friends or family where each participant is tasked with preparing a dish from a different country or culture. This fosters camaraderie and culinary exploration.

5. Travel and Food Tourism: If you have the opportunity, travel to different regions and countries to immerse yourself in their food culture. Food tourism offers a deeper understanding of the connection between cuisine and local traditions.

In closing, embrace your curiosity as the engine that drives your culinary journey. Use your mistakes as stepping stones towards growth and innovation. And, most importantly, expand your horizons by exploring diverse cuisines and cooking styles. The culinary world is vast, rich, and ever-evolving; each plate is an open invitation to a new adventure. So, embark on your gastronomic quest with an open heart and a curious mind, and let the flavors of the world inspire your culinary creations. Bon appétit!

**Setting Goals**

As you've journeyed through the previous chapters of this book, you've gained valuable insights into the world of kitchen fundamentals. You've explored essential tools, honed your skills, and embraced the spirit of culinary exploration. Now, we delve into a pivotal aspect of your culinary journey: setting goals.

Goals are the compass that guides us toward our desired destination. They provide direction, motivation, and a sense of purpose. Whether you're a novice cook looking to enhance your skills or a seasoned chef aiming to refine your expertise, setting clear culinary goals is the key to continuous improvement.

In this chapter, we'll delve into the significance of goal setting in the culinary world. We'll discuss the types of goals you can establish, from mastering specific techniques to exploring new cuisines. We'll also provide practical strategies for setting achievable goals and tracking your progress.

Your culinary journey is unique, and your goals should reflect your personal aspirations. Whether you dream of perfecting a signature dish, conquering complex cooking methods, or opening your own restaurant, this chapter will equip you with the tools and knowledge to turn your culinary dreams into reality.

So, join us as we navigate the art of setting culinary goals. Your ambitions are the driving force behind your progress, and together, we'll chart a course towards culinary excellence.

Goal setting is of significant importance in the culinary world, just as it is in any other field. Culinary professionals, whether they are chefs, cooks, bakers, or even home cooks, use goal setting to achieve their culinary aspirations and continuously improve their skills. Here are some key aspects of the significance of goal setting in the culinary world:

1. Skill Development: Culinary arts require a wide range of skills, from basic knife skills to advanced techniques in cooking, baking, and food presentation. Setting specific skill-based goals allows chefs and cooks to identify areas for improvement and work systematically to enhance their abilities.

2. Creativity and Innovation: Culinary professionals often aim to create unique and innovative dishes. Setting goals related to experimenting with new ingredients, flavors, and techniques can drive creativity and push the boundaries of traditional cooking.

3. Consistency: Consistency is essential in the culinary world, especially in restaurants and commercial kitchens. Chefs set goals for consistent quality in every dish, ensuring that each plate meets the established standards.

4. Time Management: Efficiency in the kitchen is crucial. Chefs and cooks set goals to improve their time management skills, allowing them to prepare dishes more quickly without sacrificing quality.

5. Culinary Education and Training: Many culinary professionals have goals related to furthering their education and training. This might involve attending culinary schools, workshops, or seeking mentorship from experienced chefs.

6. Menu Development: In restaurant kitchens, chefs set goals for creating and updating menus. They may aim to offer seasonal dishes, incorporate new culinary

trends, or cater to dietary preferences and restrictions.

7. Restaurant Management: Culinary entrepreneurs who own or manage restaurants often set business-related goals, such as increasing revenue, improving profitability, or expanding their culinary ventures.

8. Health and Safety: Safety and hygiene are paramount in the culinary world. Setting goals related to maintaining a clean and safe kitchen environment is essential to protect both employees and customers.

9. Customer Satisfaction: Culinary professionals aim to satisfy their customers' palates and provide a memorable dining experience. Setting goals related to customer satisfaction helps maintain a loyal clientele.

10. Competition and Awards: Many chefs and culinary artists set goals to compete in culinary competitions and earn awards or recognitions. These achievements can boost their careers and reputation.

11. Sustainability and Ethical Considerations: With the growing emphasis on sustainability and ethical food practices, chefs may set goals to source locally, reduce food waste, or incorporate sustainable ingredients into their dishes.

12. Personal Growth and Work-Life Balance: It's important for culinary professionals to set personal goals to maintain a healthy work-life balance and ensure their well-being in a high-stress industry.

In summary, goal setting is a fundamental aspect of success in the culinary world. It helps chefs and culinary enthusiasts improve their skills, maintain high standards, achieve culinary innovation, and adapt to changing trends. Whether pursuing professional excellence, running a culinary business, or exploring personal passions in the kitchen, setting and achieving culinary goals is essential for growth and advancement in the field.

**Continuous Learning**

As you are reaching the end of this book, it's essential to recognize that learning in the kitchen is an ongoing adventure, and there's always more to explore and discover.

We will now emphasize the importance of embracing a mindset that values lifelong culinary education. The culinary world is dynamic, with new trends, ingredients, and techniques constantly emerging. To stay at the forefront of this ever-evolving field and continue growing as a cook, you must be committed to continuous learning.

The Lifelong Pursuit of Culinary Education

In the culinary world, knowledge and skill are the essential ingredients that propel us forward. The art of cooking is not a static discipline; it is a living, breathing entity that constantly evolves. To thrive and excel in this ever-changing realm, it's imperative to embrace a mindset that values lifelong culinary education. Here's why this approach is of paramount importance:

Culinary Excellence Has No Finish Line

Culinary education doesn't end with a diploma or a certification. There is no summit to reach, no point of mastery where one can say, "I've learned it all." In the culinary world, the pursuit of excellence is an endless journey. Each dish, each technique, and each ingredient offers the opportunity to learn something new. Embracing a mindset of continuous learning ensures that you stay at the forefront of your craft.

Adapting to Changing Times

The culinary landscape is in a constant state of flux. New ingredients, cooking methods, dietary preferences, and culinary trends emerge regularly. By valuing lifelong culinary education, you remain adaptable and able to integrate these changes seamlessly into your repertoire. This adaptability is a hallmark of a successful chef.

Innovation and Creativity Flourish

Culinary innovation stems from a deep well of knowledge and the willingness to explore uncharted territory. A commitment to ongoing education nurtures your creative spirit, enabling you to experiment with unique flavor combinations, presentation styles, and cooking techniques. It's through these experiments that new culinary artistry is born.

Mastery of Fundamentals

Mastery of the culinary fundamentals is a critical component of any cook's journey. By dedicating yourself to lifelong culinary education, you can revisit and refine the foundational techniques that underpin all great cooking. These fundamentals, such as knife skills and sauce making, provide the solid base upon which you can build your culinary prowess.

Sharing the Joy of Culinary Discovery

Education is not a solitary pursuit. The joy of culinary discovery is best enjoyed when shared with others. As you acquire new skills and knowledge, you can pass them on to others—mentoring, teaching, or simply cooking and sharing meals with friends and family. The act of teaching and sharing deepens your own understanding and appreciation of the craft.

Resilience in the Face of Challenges

In the high-pressure world of professional kitchens, challenges are a given. Lifelong culinary education fosters resilience by preparing you to handle setbacks and crises with grace and creativity. It equips you to troubleshoot, adapt, and persevere in the face of adversity.

Personal Fulfillment

Culinary education is not just about professional growth; it's also about personal fulfillment. The satisfaction that comes from mastering a new dish, mastering a skill, or creating an exceptional meal is immeasurable. The lifelong pursuit of culinary knowledge enriches your life in countless ways.

A World of Culinary Experiences

Culinary education isn't limited to the kitchen. It's a passport to a world of culinary experiences. By valuing lifelong culinary education, you open doors to food festivals, cultural exchanges, travel, and interactions with people who share your passion.

In conclusion, the value of embracing a mindset that values lifelong culinary education cannot be overstated. It's a commitment to never-ending growth, to the art of cooking as a life's work, and to the unending joy of culinary exploration. As you continue to learn, adapt, and create, you'll find that the culinary world remains a boundless source of inspiration and fulfillment. So, savor the journey, cherish the lessons, and let your love for food be your lifelong guide. Bon appétit!

Below are some ways you can continue on your journey towards culinary excellence:

1. Take Culinary Classes:

Enroll in cooking classes at a local culinary school or community college. Many offer courses on a variety of topics, from basic cooking techniques to specialized cuisines.

Look for online cooking classes and workshops, which allow you to learn from renowned chefs and culinary experts from around the world.

2. Read Cookbooks and Culinary Literature:

Invest in a diverse collection of cookbooks, focusing on various cuisines and techniques.

Subscribe to culinary magazines and journals to stay updated on the latest trends, recipes, and cooking tips.

3. Attend Culinary Workshops and Seminars:

Participate in culinary workshops and seminars, which provide hands-on experience and insights from industry professionals.

Many food festivals and trade shows feature culinary demonstrations and educational sessions.

4. Seek Mentorship:

Find a mentor, whether it's a more experienced chef or a seasoned home cook. Learning from someone with more knowledge and experience can be invaluable.

5. Practice Regularly:

Continuously experiment with new recipes and techniques in your own kitchen. Practice is key to improving your culinary skills.

Challenge yourself with increasingly complex dishes and cooking methods.

6. Explore Different Cuisines:

Make it a goal to explore and cook dishes from various cuisines. Try recipes from different regions and cultures to broaden your culinary horizons.

7. Stay Informed About Food Trends:

Stay updated on current food trends, including plant-based cooking, sustainability, and health-conscious cuisine.

Follow culinary blogs, websites, and social media accounts dedicated to food and cooking trends.

8. Join Culinary Associations and Clubs:

Consider joining a culinary association or club in your area. These organizations often host events, offer networking opportunities, and provide access to valuable resources.

9. Travel and Taste:

Travel to different regions and countries to experience their culinary traditions and flavors firsthand. Food tourism is an immersive way to learn about different cuisines.

10. Participate in Cooking Challenges:

Engage in cooking challenges, whether it's with friends and family or through online platforms. These challenges can encourage creativity and skill development.

11. Experiment with Ingredients:

Try new and exotic ingredients in your cooking. Experimenting with unfamiliar elements can lead to culinary discoveries and broaden your flavor palate.

12. Document Your Culinary Journey:

Keep a cooking journal or blog to document your culinary experiments, successes, and lessons learned. This reflective practice can help you track your progress.

13. Collaborate and Share:

Collaborate with other culinary enthusiasts or professionals on cooking projects, events, or recipe development. Sharing ideas and knowledge can be mutually beneficial.

14. Consider Advanced Training:

If you're looking to pursue a career in the culinary field, consider more formal training, such as enrolling in a culinary school, pursuing a culinary degree, or earning professional certifications.

15. Stay Open-Minded and Humble:

Always approach learning with an open mind. Be receptive to feedback and be willing to adapt your techniques and ideas.

Don't be discouraged by culinary mishaps or setbacks; view them as learning opportunities.

Remember that the culinary world is vast and diverse, and there is always something new to learn. The key is to maintain a passion for cooking, a spirit of exploration, and a commitment to continuous improvement. Whether you're a professional chef or a home cook, the journey of culinary learning is both enriching and rewarding.

**Conclusion**

As we arrive at the end of this book, it's a moment to reflect on the culinary voyage you've embarked upon. Throughout this comprehensive guide, we've ventured into the heart of the kitchen, exploring the tools, techniques, and practices that lay the groundwork for culinary mastery. We've journeyed from the basics to the advanced, from essential tools to specialized gadgets, and from fundamental skills to efficient techniques.

In this Conclusion, we bring together all the knowledge, skills, and insights you've gained along this culinary expedition. It's an opportunity to consolidate your understanding and appreciate the significance of what you've learned.

We've covered a wide range of topics, from knives to cookware, from utensils to specialized tools, and from efficient cooking practices to budget-friendly kitchen setups. You've discovered not just the "how" but also the "why" behind various culinary practices.

Throughout this journey, we've emphasized the value of continuous learning and experimentation in the kitchen. Cooking is not a static endeavor; it's a dynamic art that invites exploration and innovation. By continuously seeking new experiences, flavors, and techniques, you'll not only become a more skilled cook but also find deeper joy in the creative process of preparing meals.

As you conclude this book, remember that the kitchen is your canvas, and your tools are your brushes. Every dish you create is a masterpiece waiting to be explored. Whether you're an aspiring chef or a seasoned home cook, there is always room for growth and refinement in the culinary world.

So, with a heart full of passion and a mind filled with knowledge, step out into your kitchen and continue your culinary journey. Share your creations with loved ones, explore new cuisines, and let your kitchen be the stage for your culinary adventures.

We hope this book has served as a valuable guide on your path to becoming a confident and skilled cook. As you close this chapter, remember that the culinary world is boundless, and the joy of cooking is limitless. Keep exploring, keep learning, and keep savoring the delicious moments that the kitchen has to offer.

Bon Appetit, and may your culinary journey be as vibrant and diverse as the flavors of the world!

# Appendix

## Essential Kitchen Tools Checklist

Use this checklist to ensure you have all the essential kitchen tools you need for efficient and enjoyable cooking.

### Knives

Chef's Knife: Versatile for chopping, slicing, and dicing.

Paring Knife: Ideal for precise tasks like peeling and trimming.

Serrated Knife: Perfect for slicing bread and delicate items.

Utility Knife: Handy for various cutting tasks.

Honing Rod: For keeping your knives sharp.

### Cutting Boards

Wooden Cutting Board: Great for knife longevity.

Plastic Cutting Board: Easy to clean and dishwasher safe.

Bamboo Cutting Board: Sustainable and durable.

### Measuring Cups and Spoons

Dry Measuring Cups: For ingredients like flour and sugar.

Liquid Measuring Cups: For liquids such as milk and oil.

Measuring Spoons: Precise measurements for spices and extracts.

### Cooking Pans and Sheets

Skillet/Frying Pan: Versatile for frying, sautéing, and more.

Saucepan: Ideal for soups, sauces, and boiling liquids.

Baking Sheet: For cookies, biscuits, and flat baked goods.

Loaf Pan: Perfect for bread and loaf-shaped cakes.

Pie Pan: Used for baking pies and quiches.

## Cooking Utensils

Spatula: For flipping and lifting delicate foods.

Tongs: Versatile for gripping and serving various items.

Ladle: Essential for serving soups and stews.

## Specialized Tools

Blender: For smoothies, soups, and sauces.

Food Processor: Great for chopping, slicing, and mixing.

Toaster: Quick for toasting bread and breakfast items.

Peeler: Handy for peeling fruits and vegetables.

Zester: Adds citrusy flavor with zest.

Can Opener: Essential for opening canned ingredients.

## Cleaning and Maintenance

Sharpening Tools: To keep your knives sharp.

Kitchen Towels: For keeping your workspace clean.

Cleaning Supplies: Mild dish soap, non-abrasive scrubbers, etc.

## Efficiency Tools

Timer: Helps you keep track of cooking times.

Thermometer: Ensures food safety and precision.

Cutting Mats: Protect your countertops and improve hygiene.

Remember to choose tools that align with your cooking style and preferences. Happy cooking!

**Knife Skills Practice Exercises**

1. Julienne Cut Practice:

- Start with a carrot or cucumber.

- Peel and trim the ends.

- Cut it into even strips about 1/8 inch thick.

- Aim for uniformity in size and shape.

2. Mincing Garlic Practice:

- Peel a garlic clove.

- Position the knife over the garlic.

- Use a rocking motion to finely mince the garlic.

3. Chiffonade Basil Practice:

- Stack fresh basil leaves on top of each other.

- Roll them tightly.

- Slice across the rolled basil into thin strips.

4. Dice Onion Practice:

- Cut off the top of an onion and cut it in half.

- Peel one half and make horizontal and vertical cuts without cutting through the root.

- Finally, make downward cuts to dice the onion.

5. Slicing Tomatoes Practice:

- Slice a tomato into thin, even slices.

- Aim for slices of consistent thickness.

6. Peeling Practice:

-Take a potato or apple.

-Use a paring knife to peel it, removing the skin evenly without wasting too much flesh.

7. Supreme Citrus Practice:

- Cut off the top and bottom of an orange or grapefruit.

- Following the curve of the fruit, carefully remove the peel and pith.

- Segment the citrus by slicing between the membranes.

8. Butterfly Chicken Breast Practice:

- Lay a boneless, skinless chicken breast flat on your cutting board.

- Slice horizontally through the thickest part, stopping just before cutting it in half.

- Open the breast like a book to create a butterfly shape.

9. Fine Herb Chopping Practice:

- Gather fresh herbs like parsley, cilantro, or chives.

- Hold them together and chop finely using a rocking motion.

10. Carve a Roasted Chicken Practice:

 - Roast a whole chicken and let it rest.

 - Carve the chicken into portions, following the natural joints.

These exercises will help you improve your knife skills and become more confident in the kitchen. Practice regularly, and you'll be dicing, slicing, and chopping like a pro in no time!

**Volume Conversion Chart**

1 cup (c) = 8 fluid ounces (fl. oz) = 240 milliliters (ml)

1 tablespoon (tbsp) = 0.5 fluid ounces (fl. oz) = 15 milliliters (ml)

1 teaspoon (tsp) = 0.17 fluid ounces (fl. oz) = 5 milliliters (ml)

**Weight Conversion Chart**

1 pound (lb.) = 16 ounces (oz) = 453.592 grams (g)

1 ounce (oz) = 28.35 grams (g)

1 kilogram (kg) = 2.205 pounds (lb.) = 1000 grams (g)

**Temperature Conversion Chart**

°F to °C: Subtract 32, then multiply by 5/9

°C to °F: Multiply by 9/5, then add 32

-10°C = 14°F

0°C = 32°F (freezing point of water)

100°C = 212°F (boiling point of water)

**Oven Temperature Conversion Chart**

Very Slow or Very Low: 225°F - 275°F (107°C - 135°C)

Slow or Low: 300°F - 325°F (149°C - 163°C)

Moderate or Medium: 350°F - 375°F (177°C - 190°C)

Hot or High: 400°F - 450°F (204°C - 232°C)

Very Hot or Very High: 475°F and above (246°C and above)

**Cup to Gram Conversion for Common Ingredients**

All-Purpose Flour:

1 cup = 120 grams

Granulated Sugar:

1 cup = 200 grams

Brown Sugar (packed):

1 cup = 220 grams

Butter:

1 cup = 227 grams

Milk:

1 cup = 240 milliliters = 240 grams (for water-based liquids)

These conversion charts should help your readers easily convert between different units of measurement when following recipes or cooking in the kitchen.

# Recipes to Get You Started

**Classic Spaghetti Carbonara**

**Ingredients:**

- 8 ounces (about 225 grams) of spaghetti

- 2 large eggs

- 1 cup (about 100 grams) of grated Pecorino Romano cheese

- 4 ounces (about 115 grams) of pancetta or guanciale, diced

- 2 cloves of garlic, minced

- Salt and black pepper, to taste

- Fresh parsley, chopped (for garnish)

**Instructions:**

1. Cook the spaghetti in a large pot of salted boiling water until al dente. Drain and set aside.

2. In a separate bowl, whisk together the eggs, grated cheese, and a pinch of black pepper.

3. In a skillet, sauté the diced pancetta or guanciale until it becomes crispy. Add minced garlic and cook for another minute.

4. Remove the skillet from heat and add the cooked spaghetti. Toss to combine.

5. Quickly pour the egg and cheese mixture over the hot pasta and toss vigorously. The heat from the pasta will cook the eggs, creating a creamy sauce.

6. Season with additional black pepper and garnish with chopped fresh parsley. Serve immediately.

## Easy Tomato and Basil Bruschetta

### Ingredients:

- 4-6 slices of rustic bread
- 2 ripe tomatoes, diced
- 1-2 cloves of garlic, minced
- Fresh basil leaves, chopped
- Extra-virgin olive oil
- Balsamic vinegar (optional)
- Salt and pepper, to taste

### Instructions:

1. Toast the bread slices until they are golden brown and crispy.
2. In a bowl, combine diced tomatoes, minced garlic, and chopped basil.
3. Drizzle with extra-virgin olive oil and, if desired, a splash of balsamic vinegar for added flavor.
4. Season with salt and pepper and mix everything together.
5. Spoon the tomato mixture onto the toasted bread slices.
6. Serve as an appetizer or snack.

**Homemade Guacamole**

**Ingredients:**

- 2 ripe avocados

- 1 small red onion, finely diced

- 1-2 cloves of garlic, minced

- 1-2 ripe tomatoes, diced

- Fresh cilantro leaves, chopped

- Juice of 1 lime

- Salt and pepper, to taste

- Jalapeño pepper (optional, for heat)

**Instructions:**

1. Cut the avocados in half, remove the pits, and scoop the flesh into a bowl.

2. Mash the avocados with a fork until you reach your desired level of chunkiness.

3. Add diced red onion, minced garlic, diced tomatoes, and chopped cilantro to the mashed avocado.

4. Squeeze the juice of one lime over the mixture and stir to combine.

5. If you like a bit of heat, finely chop a small amount of jalapeño pepper and add it to the guacamole.

6. Season with salt and pepper to taste.

7. Serve with tortilla chips or as a topping for tacos and burritos.

**One-Pot Chicken and Rice**

**Ingredients:**

- 1 cup of rice

- 2 boneless, skinless chicken breasts, diced

- 1 onion, diced

- 2 cloves of garlic, minced

- 1 red bell pepper, diced

- 1 cup of frozen peas

- 2 cups of chicken broth

- 1 teaspoon of paprika

- Salt and pepper, to taste

- Olive oil for cooking

**Instructions:**

1. In a large skillet or pot, heat a drizzle of olive oil over medium-high heat.

2. Add diced chicken and cook until browned on all sides. Remove the chicken from the pan and set it aside.

3. In the same pan, add diced onion and cook until it becomes translucent.

4. Add minced garlic, diced red bell pepper, and rice. Stir and cook for a few minutes until the rice is lightly toasted.

5. Return the cooked chicken to the pan.

6. Pour in chicken broth and add frozen peas and paprika.

7. Season with salt and pepper to taste.

8. Cover the pan, reduce the heat to low, and simmer for 20-25 minutes or until the rice is cooked and the liquid is absorbed.

9. Fluff the rice with a fork, and it's ready to serve.

**Baked Lemon Herb Salmon**

**Ingredients:**

- 2 salmon fillets

- 2 tablespoons of olive oil

- Juice and zest of 1 lemon

- 2 cloves of garlic, minced

- Fresh herbs (e.g., dill, parsley, or thyme), chopped

- Salt and pepper, to taste

- Lemon slices (for garnish)

**Instructions:**

1. Preheat your oven to 375°F (190°C).

2. In a small bowl, whisk together olive oil, lemon juice, lemon zest, minced garlic, chopped fresh herbs, salt, and pepper.

3. Place the salmon fillets on a baking sheet lined with parchment paper or foil.

4. Brush the lemon herb mixture generously over the salmon.

5. Arrange lemon slices on top for extra flavor and garnish.

6. Bake in the preheated oven for about 15-20 minutes, or until the salmon flakes easily with a fork.

7. Serve your baked lemon herb salmon with your choice of sides, such as roasted vegetables or rice.


These beginner-friendly recipes cover a range of cuisines and cooking techniques to help new cooks gain confidence in the kitchen.

**Pineapple Upside Down Cake Recipe:**

For the topping:

- 1/4 cup (1/2 stick) unsalted butter

- 3/4 cup brown sugar, packed

- 7-8 pineapple rings (fresh or canned)

- Maraschino cherries (optional)

For the cake:

- 1 1/2 cups all-purpose flour

- 1 1/2 teaspoons baking powder

- 1/4 teaspoon salt

- 1/2 cup (1 stick) unsalted butter, softened

- 1 cup granulated sugar

- 2 large eggs

- 1 teaspoon vanilla extract

- 1/2 cup pineapple juice (from the canned pineapple)

- 1/4 cup whole milk

Instructions:

1. Preheat your oven to 350°F (175°C).

2. In a 9-inch round cake pan, melt the 1/4 cup of butter in the oven. Once melted, remove the pan from the oven and sprinkle the brown sugar evenly over the melted butter.

3. Arrange the pineapple rings on top of the brown sugar in a decorative pattern. You can place a Maraschino cherry in the center of each pineapple ring if desired.

4. In a separate bowl, whisk together the flour, baking powder, and salt. Set this dry mixture aside.

5. In another bowl, cream together the softened butter and granulated sugar until light and fluffy.

6. Add the eggs one at a time, beating well after each addition. Stir in the vanilla extract.

7. Gradually mix in the dry ingredients, alternating with the pineapple juice and milk, beginning and ending with the dry ingredients. Mix until just combined.

8. Pour the cake batter over the pineapple topping in the cake pan, spreading it evenly.

9. Bake in the preheated oven for 40-45 minutes or until a toothpick inserted into the center of the cake comes out clean.

10. Allow the cake to cool in the pan for about 5 minutes, then carefully invert it onto a serving plate. Be cautious, as the pan and topping will be hot.

11. Let the cake cool completely before serving. Slice, serve, and enjoy your homemade Pineapple Upside Down Cake!

**Honey Garlic Chicken**

**Ingredients:**

For the Chicken:

4 boneless, skinless chicken breasts

3 tsp. Granulated Garlic

3 tsp. Onion Powder

1 tsp. Paprika

1 tsp. Salt

1 tsp. Black Pepper

2 cups of All-purpose flour (for coating)

Vegetable Oil (for frying)

For the Honey Garlic Sauce:

1/2 cup honey

1/4 cup soy sauce

2 tablespoons finely chopped fresh parsley.

1 teaspoon minced garlic

1/2 teaspoon grated fresh ginger (optional)

1/4 teaspoon red pepper flakes (adjust to taste)

Instructions:

### 1. Prepare the Chicken:

Cut the chicken breast into tender or bite size pieces. In a small bowl mix all seasonings until well blended. Season the chicken breasts with half of the seasoning mixture on both sides. Add the other half to the flour. Coat the chicken with flour mixture and set aside.

### 2. Fry the Chicken:

Heat the oil in a large skillet over medium-high heat.

Add the chicken breasts to the skillet and cook for about 6-8 minutes on each side or until they are cooked through and have a nice golden-brown color on the outside.

Remove the chicken from the skillet and set it aside.

### 3. Prepare the Honey Garlic Sauce:

In a saucepan, add the honey, soy sauce, minced garlic, grated ginger (if using), and red pepper flakes.

Cook the sauce over medium heat, stirring continuously, for about 2-3 minutes until it thickens slightly and combines well.

### 4. Combine Chicken and Sauce:

Add chicken to the honey garlic sauce.

Spoon the sauce over the chicken and allow it to simmer for a couple of minutes, ensuring the chicken is coated in the sauce.

5. Serve:

Sprinkle freshly chopped parsley over the chicken.

Serve the honey garlic chicken hot, with steamed rice or your favorite side dishes.

Enjoy your homemade honey garlic chicken! It's a perfect balance of sweet and savory flavors.

## Acknowledgments

As I embarked on the journey of creating "Mastering Kitchen Fundamentals," I encountered numerous challenges and a few unexpected obstacles along the way. However, I am immensely grateful to the many individuals who supported me throughout this culinary adventure. Their unwavering encouragement and assistance have been invaluable.

First and foremost, I want to express my deepest gratitude to Jehovah GOD for blessing me with life and the intellectual capacity to absorb the wealth of knowledge that has shaped this cookbook. Without divine guidance and inspiration, this project would not have been possible.

I owe a special debt of gratitude to my mother, Regina Alexander, whose early introduction to the world of cooking ignited my passion for the culinary arts. Her guidance, love, and unwavering support have been a constant source of motivation on this journey.

To my beloved wife, Shanae, and our wonderful children, Shanequa, Autumn, Raymone Jr., Essence, Raekwon, Ray'Sean, and Rayzair, I want to express my deepest appreciation. Your love, patience, and understanding have sustained me through the long hours in the kitchen and the countless recipe experiments. You are the driving force behind my perseverance, even when it feels like I'm swimming against the current.

I am also thankful for the countless friends, mentors, and fellow food enthusiasts who have shared their culinary wisdom, insights, and inspiration with me over the years. Your collective contributions have enriched this cookbook and made it a comprehensive guide to mastering the art of cooking.

Finally, I extend my heartfelt appreciation to all the readers and aspiring chefs who will embark on their own culinary journeys with "Mastering Kitchen Fundamentals." It is my hope that this cookbook serves as a reliable companion on your path to culinary excellence.

Thank you, from the bottom of my heart, for being a part of this delicious adventure.

With gratitude and a passion for great food,

Raymone Keitt

About the Author: Raymone Keitt

Raymone Keitt's culinary journey is a story of passion, perseverance, and a relentless pursuit of culinary excellence. Born and raised in the vibrant heart of Brooklyn, New York, Raymone's love for cooking was sparked by the precious moments spent in the kitchen with his mother. Their shared kitchen adventures were the foundation upon which he built his remarkable culinary career.

From the tender age of seven, Raymone exhibited a remarkable talent for cooking, preparing whole meals for his mother and four siblings. As the middle child in a family that faced its fair share of challenges, he grew up without fully understanding the extent of their struggles, thanks to his mother's remarkable ability to shield them from adversity. Nevertheless, this nurturing environment kindled the fire of Raymone's culinary passion.

Raymone's culinary journey was a constant evolution, a journey of experimentation that led to a wealth of experience. He courageously delved into the kitchen, experimenting with ingredients, sometimes with delicious outcomes and occasionally with less favorable ones. Yet, it was through these trials and errors that he honed his skills and refined his culinary talents.

His first step into the professional culinary world came with a position at Sheppard's Pie, a family-owned catering company owned by Pat and Byron Sheppard. In a relatively short period of time, Raymone was entrusted with the monumental task of independently catering and hosting an entire wedding reception. This experience became a defining moment, showcasing his unwavering strength and culinary proficiency while opening his eyes to a world of limitless possibilities.

Since his time at Sheppard's Pie, Raymone has successfully catered hundreds of events, ranging from elegant gatherings to lively barbecues and cherished family functions. His delectable creations have won over not only the hearts of his friends and family but also his local community.

Now, adding a new chapter to his culinary journey, Raymone proudly takes on the role of a cookbook author. "Mastering Kitchen Fundamentals: The Beginner's Guide to Culinary Excellence" is a testament to his expertise and his dedication to sharing the essential skills and techniques required to thrive in the kitchen. Raymone's desire to empower budding chefs with the knowledge he has acquired shines through in this book.

While Raymone's journey is far from complete, he envisions a future that includes the opening of a restaurant and a food truck, promising even more delightful culinary experiences to savor. With role models like Emeril Lagasse, Bobby Flay, Rachael Ray, The Neelys, Guy Fieri, and an array of Food Network stars lighting his path, Raymone Keitt continues to inspire and guide others on their own culinary adventures.

Prepare to embark on a culinary journey of your own with "Mastering Kitchen Fundamentals." Raymone's story is a testament to the transformative power of the kitchen, where dreams are forged, struggles are overcome, and delicious memories are created. His passion and expertise will guide you toward your own culinary excellence, making your kitchen the heart of your home.

Stay tuned, as Raymone Keitt's journey is far from over—his restaurant and food truck are on the horizon. Watch out for this rising culinary star!

# Index

A Call to Adventure **49**

A World of Culinary Experiences **55**

About the Author **77-78**

Acknowledgments **76**

Adapting to Changing Times **54**

Appendix **60**

Baked Lemon Herb Salmon **70**

Bamboo cutting boards **16, 60**

Benefits of Choosing the Right Cooking Utensils **32**

Blender Efficiency **40**

Budget Planning **46**

Budget-Friendly Alternatives **44**

Budget-Friendly Kitchen Setup **43**

Building Your Essential Toolkit **7**

Can Opener **32, 34**

Chicken Marsala **29**

Chickpea and Vegetable Stir-Fry **45**

Choosing the Right Cooking Utensils **32**

Choosing the Right Cutting Board **17**

Classic Spaghetti Carbonara **66**

Classic Tomato Soup **28**

Cleaning and Maintenance **37, 61**

Cooking Pans and Sheets **26**

Cookware Choices **44**

Cookware Efficiency **41**

Culinary excellence has no finish line **54**

Culinary Exploration **47**

Cup to Gram Conversion **65**

Cutting Boards **14-18, 60**

Dishwasher-Safe Tools **39**

DIY Solutions **44**

Easy Tomato and Basil Bruschetta **67**

Efficiency Techniques **40**

Embracing Curiosity, Mistakes, and Culinary Diversity **48, 49**

Essential Cooking Utensils **31**

Essential Kitchen Tools **5**

Establishing a Cleaning Routine **39**

Experimentation: The Heart of Discovery **48**

Factors to Consider When Choosing a Pan **27**

Flexible mats **17**

From Fork to Farm **49**

Garlic Press **35**

Glass or stone cutting boards **16**

Homemade Guacamole **68**

Honey Garlic Chicken **73-75**

Honing vs. Sharpening: Keeping Your Knives in Top Shape **13**

Identifying Essential Kitchen Tools **43**

Ingredient-Based Cooking **45**

Innovation and Creativity Flourish **54**

Investing in Quality: Why It Matters **6**

Kitchen Scale **36**

Knife Efficiency **40**

Knife Skills **11-13**

Knife Skills Practice Exercises **62**

Knives **11-13, 60**

Local Bounty and Seasonal Sensibility **48**

Maintaining Tools for Efficiency **41**

Mastery of Fundamentals **54**

Measuring Cups and Spoons **19-23, 60**

Meat Tenderizer **35**

Mixing Bowls **23**

Mortar and Pestle **37**

One-Pot Chicken and Rice **69**

Optional Utensils for Aspiring Chefs **9, 33**

Organized Workspace **42**

Oven Temperature Conversion Chart **65**

Pan-Seared Salmon with Lemon Butter Sauce **28**

Peeler **32, 34**

Personal Fulfillment **55**

Pineapple Upside Down Cake **71**

Pizza Cutter **35**

Plastic cutting boards **15**

Preserving Tradition, Creating Innovation **48**

Recipes to Get You Started **66**

Resilience in the Face of Challenges **55**

Saucepan **26**

Sauté Pan **27**

Setting Goals **51**

Sharing the Joy of Culinary Discovery **55**

Skillet (Frying Pan) **26**

Special Care for Knives **39**

Specialized kitchen tools **34, 61**

Stainless Steel **37**

Temperature Conversion Chart **64**

The Final Course **47**

The Importance of Efficiency **40**

The Journey Is the Destination **49**

The Lifelong Pursuit of Culinary Education **54**

The Must-Have Cooking Utensils **31**

The Virtue of Curiosity **49**

Understanding the Role of Cooking Utensils **31**

Unleash Your Inner Explorer **48**

Volume Conversion Chart **64**

Weight Conversion Chart **64**

Whisk **32**

Wooden cutting boards **15, 17**

Wooden Spoon **32**

Zester **34**

*Black Steel's Kitchen*

Made in the USA
Columbia, SC
15 January 2024

307e1c34-f1ab-44f6-a982-910a36e76723R01